WARLORD

IN

THE

WAR ROOM

OF FIRE

By Tella Olayeri

08023583168

TELLA OLAYERI

All rights reserved. No part of this publication may be reproduced, stored in a retrieval system or transmitted in any form or by any means electronics, mechanical, photocopying, recording, or otherwise, without the prior written permission of the publisher, in accordance with the provisions of the copyright Act.

Any person who does any unauthorized act in relation to this publication may be liable to criminal prosecution and civil claims for damages. It is protected under the copyright laws.

Published By:
GOD'S LINK VENTURES

Email tellaolayeri@gmail.com

Website http://tellaolayeri.com

US Contact
Ruth Jack
14 Milewood Road
Verbank
N.Y.12585
U.S.A. +19176428989

APPRECIATION

I give special appreciation to my wife MRS NGOZI OLAYERI for her assistance in ensuring that this book is published and our children that played around us to encourage us day and night.

Also, this manuscript wouldn't have seen the light of the day, if not for the spiritual encouragement I gathered from my father in the Lord, Dr. D.K. OLUKOYA who served as spiritual mirror that brightens my hope to explore my calling (Evangelism).

We shall all reap our blessings in heaven but the battle to make heaven is not over, until it is won.

PREFACE

Warlords are soldiers in the battle field. They don't give room for nonsense. They hate being in the defensive but take the battle to the gate of enemy. Christian soldiers are warlords. They take the bull by the horn. They hardly misfire, they don't waste bullet in prayer. They go straight to the point, aim at the enemy and scatter his plans. Warlords are not lazy soldiers; they wake at night to pray. Morning Prayer is food to them. They never slumber or pray unguided prayer. When it is time to praise God, they do it perfectly well. They praise God until heavens open.

These are the acts you must display when you hold this book to pray. As a warlord, pick songs of your choice, praise God, let heaven open. Praise God who fights battle in praises. Always know one thing, the battle is not yours but of God. When Moab and Amnon rose against Israel, King Jehoshaphat won the battle in praises. 2 Chronicles 20:22. Moab and Amnon may represet strangers who are out to take what belongs to you. They want to humiliate you and take you captive. They want to disgrace you and put you to shame. The Lord we serve says, shame and disgrace is not your portion.

Let it be known to you today, any power that rise to oppose your prosperity shall be silenced. You may have ancestral problem troubling your lineage, it shall seize, because the Lord made you a warlord to shoot arrows in the war room. Your parent may tell you, the problem was there before you were born. They say, it is older than you. This is human judgment, not one from heavenly throne.

No matter their number, gang up or any form they shall fail. The Lord says, no power shall empty you. You are born great, a soldier, warlord, a General in the battle field. Do you know, a General doesn't fear going to battle? Fear not stand firm, and see what the Lord shall do for you today.

The battle line is drawn; the Lord is on your side. Pick this book. Have the spirit of, I shall win and be great. You are born great, and shall be great. As a warlord, be spirit filled with faith. You are a winner. Pick this book and fire on. Good-luck.

GOOD NEWS!!!

My audiobook is now available, to get one visit acx.com and search **"Tella Olayeri."**

Brethren, to be loaded and reloaded visit: *amazon.com/author/tellaolayeri* for a full spiritual sojourn for my books.

Thanks.

PREVIOUS PUBLICATIONS OF THE AUTHOR

1. 100% CONFESSIONS and PROPHECIES to Locate Helpers and helpers to locate you
2. 1000 Prayer Points for Children Breakthrough
3. 1010 (One Thousand and Ten) DREAMS and Interpretations
4. 2000 Dangerous Prayer for First Born
5. 365 DREAMS and INTERPRETATIONS
6. 430 Prayers to Cancel Bad Dreams and Overcome Witchcraft Powers part one (DREAMS AND YOU Book 1)
7. 430 Prayers to Claim Good Dreams and Overcome Witchcraft Powers part two (DREAMS AND YOU Book 2)
8. 630 Acidic Prayers: With Missile Prayer for Speedy Breakthrough, Healing and Deliverance
9. 650 DREAMS AND INTERPRETATIONS
10. 700 Prayers to Clear Unemployment Out of Your Way
11. 720 Missile Prayers that Silence Enemies: Prayers that Bring Peace and Rest
12. 740 Rocket Prayers that Break Satanic Embargo
13. 777 Deliverance Prayers for Healing and Breakthrough
14. 800 Deliverance Prayer for Middle Born: Daily Devotional for Teen and Adult

15. <u>800 Deliverance Prayer Points for First Born: Daily Devotional for Teen and Adult</u>
16. <u>800 Deliverance Prayer Points for Last Born: Daily Devotional for Teen and Adult</u>
17. <u>830 Prophecies for the Head: Deliverance Prayer Book for the Brain, Eye, Ear and Mouth</u>
18. <u>Acidic Prayer against Dream Killers</u>
19. <u>Anointing for Eleventh Hour Help: Hope and Help for Your Turbulent Times</u>
20. <u>Atomic Decree that Opens Great Doors</u>
21. <u>Atomic Prayers that Destroy Destiny Killers</u>
22. <u>Atomic Prayers that Destroy Witchcraft Powers and Silence Enemies</u>
23. <u>Biblical Prayer against Sickness and Diseases: Winning the Battle Against Diseases</u>
24. <u>Calling God to Silence Witchcraft Powers: Prayers That Rout Demons</u>
25. <u>Children Deliverance: Power of a Praying Parent</u>
26. <u>COMMAND the DAY: 365 Days of Prayer for Christian that Bring Calm & Peace</u>
27. <u>Command The Night 30 Days Spiritual Manual Prayer Book: A Devotional Prayer Book With 1,200 Violent Prayer Points For Healing Breakthrough and Divine Acceleration</u>
28. <u>Command the Night Against 100 types of Witchcraft Arrows: Powerful Prayers in the War Room</u>

29. Command the Night Against Battles of Life: Prayers That Rout Demons
30. COMMAND the Night deal with Witchcraft Powers and be set free: Know Your Enemy and Be More Than a Conqueror (SERIOUS MIDNIGHT BATTLE Book 2)
31. Command the Night with 370 Prayers against Deadly Arrows that Bury Destiny
32. Command the Night With 444 Prophetic Prayers to move from the Valley to Mountain Top: A Guide to Scripture-Based Prayer
33. Command the Night with 90 Decrees and Prophecies: Know Your Enemy and Be More Than a Conqueror (SERIOUS MIDNIGHT BATTLE Book 1)
34. COMMAND the YEAR: 365 Days Atomic Prayer Journal for Christian that Silence Enemies and Bring Peace
35. Command Your Marriage: The Love Language for Couples
36. Dangerous Decree and Prophecies part one: Powerful Prayers in the War Room
37. Dangerous Prayer Against Strange Women: O Lord, Save My Marriage from Wrecking And Divorce
38. Dangerous Prayer that makes Satan Flee and surrender your possession: Powerful Prayer that Makes Satan Helpless
39. Deliverance from Spirit of Dog

40. Deliverance Prayer For Last Born: Daily Devotional for Teen and Adult
41. Deliverance Prayer for Middle Born: Daily Devotional for Teen and Adult
42. Deliverance Prayers for First Born: Daily Devotional for Teen and Adult
43. Dictionary of Dreams: The Dream Interpretation Dictionary With Symbols, Signs, and Meanings
44. Double Fire Double Thunder Prayer Book
45. Dreams and Visions and ways to Understand their Mysterious Meanings part one: The Dream Interpretation Dictionary Containing Symbols, Signs, and Meanings (DREAMS INTERPRETATION Book 1)
46. Dreams and Visions and ways to Understand their Mysterious Meanings part three: With Dreams Containing Symbols, Signs, Colors, Numbers and Meanings (DREAMS INTERPRETATION Book 3)
47. Dreams and Visions and ways to Understand their Mysterious Meanings part two: The Dream Interpretation Dictionary Containing Symbols, Signs, and Meanings (DREAMS INTERPRETATION Book 2)
48. Enough of Sudden Diseases and Infirmities: With Biblical Secrets to Divine Healing against Strange Sickness, Pains, Diseases and Infirmities
49. Fire for Fire part one: (PRAYER BOOK Book 1)

50. Fire for Fire part two: Prayers That Rout Demons (PRAYER BOOK Book 2)
51. Fury Fire Fury Thunder: That Gives Instant Solution To Challenges Of Life
52. Goliath at the Gate of Marriage
53. I am not Alone Jesus is With Me
54. I Decree Fire To Consume And Destroy Witchcraft Powers
55. I Fire You: Learning to Pray like a Powerful Prayer Warrior (PRAYER BOOK Book 1)
56. I Shall Excel: A Guide to Scripture-Based Prayer
57. It is War!: Declare Your Enemies Defeated And Destroy Them
58. Lightning And Thunder Prayer Book
59. My Head is not for Sale: Prayers That Rout Demons
60. My Marriage shall not break: The Secret to Love and Marriage That Lasts
61. My Well of Honey Shall not dry
62. NAKED Warriors
63. Prayer After Dream: Take Charge Of Your Dream While You Wake
64. Prayer Against Sex In The Dream
65. Prayer Against Untimely Death
66. Prayer Against Witchcraft Dream And Storm Of Darkness
67. Prayer For Fruit Of The Womb: Expecting Mothers

68. Prayer For Pregnant Women: With All Christian Names And Meanings
69. Prayer For Singles: Preparing My Heart For Marriage By Praying
70. Prayer For Youths And Teenagers: Daily Devotional For Teen And Adult
71. Prayer In Time Of Emergency: God Helps In Time Of Need
72. Prayer That Makes Enemy Surrender
73. Prayer That Scatter Witchcraft Agenda
74. Prayer To Break The Head Of The Dragon
75. Prayer To Locate Helpers And Helpers To Locate You
76. Prayer to Make Wealth and Sink Poverty part one (WEALTH CREATION BOOK Book 1)
77. Prayer to Make Wealth and Sink Poverty part two (WEALTH CREATION BOOK Book 2)
78. Prayer To Pray When Debtors Owe You And Refuse To Pay
79. Prayer to Remember Dreams
80. Prayer to Secure Golden Breakthrough Job
81. Prayer to Silence Financial Crises: Everything You Need to Start Making Money Today
82. Prayer When All Seems Lost: Finding Unexpected Strength When Disappointments Leave You Shattered
83. Prayers to Retain Jobs and Excel in Office
84. Praying Through Pandemic and Receive Solution

85. Shake Heaven with Prayer and Praises
86. Shut Up! Thou Pit Of Hell
87. Silencing the Wickedness of the Wicked with Dangerous Decree
88. Strange Women! Leave my Husband Alone: The Secret to Love and Marriage That Lasts
89. Thunder and Fire Prayers That Scatter Witchcraft Activities
90. Thunder Prayer That Provokes Angelic Violence Against Works Of Darkness
91. Thunder Prayers that Break Satanic Covenant
92. Tongue Of Fire And Warfare Deliverance
93. Total Body Deliverance: Powerful Prophetic Prayers & Declarations For Divine Healing
94. Victory over Satanic House Part One: Ridding Your Home Of Spiritual Darkness
95. Victory over Satanic House Part Two: Ridding Your Home Of Spiritual Darkness
96. War Lords In The War Room Of Fire
97. Warfare in the Office: Prayer to Silence Tough Times in Office
98. Warfare Prayer Against Satanic Dream

See all at: amazon.com/author/tellaolayeri

TELLA OLAYERI

Table of Contents

PRAYER TO TERMINATE WITCHCRAFT STRANGERS 15

I REBUKE DISGRACE AND SHAME...24

O LORD SILENCE POWERS OPPOSING PROSPERITY IN MY LIFE .33

I OVERCOME POWERS OLDER THAN ME 41

WITCHCRAFT POWER ASSIGN TO EMPTY ME SHALL FAIL 50

CHAPTER 1

PRAYER TO TERMINATE WITCHCRAFT STRANGERS

Psalm 18:43-44

43. You have delivered me from the attacks of the people; you have made me the head of nations. People I did not know are subject to me,

44. As soon as they hear me, they obey me; foreigners cringe before me.

Psalm 1:4-6

4. Not so the wicked! They are like chaff that the wind blows away.

5. Therefore the wicked will not stand in the judgment, nor sinners in the assembly of the righteous.

6. For the LORD watches over the way of the righteous, but the way of the wicked leads to destruction.

Psalm 54:1-5

1. Save me, O God, by your name; vindicate me by your might.

2. Hear my prayer, O God; listen to the words of my mouth.

3. Strangers are attacking me; ruthless men seek my life- men without regard for God.

4. Surely God is my help; the Lord is the one who sustains me.

5. Let evil recoil on those who slander me; in your faithfulness destroy them.

PRAYER POINTS

1. I thank you Lord for your protection over me, in the name of Jesus.
2. O Lord, I praise you for your power surpassing greatness in the name of Jesus.
3. I thank you Lord for keeping me in perfect peace, in the name of Jesus.
4. O Lord, have mercy upon me, in the name of Jesus.
5. O Lord, lay your hand of forgiveness upon me, in the name of Jesus.
6. Lord Jesus, I repent of my sins before you, forgive me O Lord, by your power.

7. I cover myself with blood of Jesus against strange powers around me, in the name of Jesus.
8. I drink blood of Jesus, to purge me of evil deposit in my body, in the name of Jesus.
9. Holy Spirit, create conducive environment for me where witchcraft stranger will have no place, in the name of Jesus.
10. Holy Spirit Divine, lift me above witchcraft strangers, in the name of Jesus.
11. Holy Ghost Fire, set me free from strange power, in the name of Jesus.
12. Witchcraft arrangement of witches and wizards to bury my talent, scatter, in the name of Jesus.
13. Spiritual strongman in charge of my life, leave me alone and die, in the name of Jesus.
14. Every ancestral covenant with strange power break, in the name of Jesus.
15. Heavenly hands of fire, separate me from dark strangers, in the name of Jesus.
16. Satanic altar, giving power to strange powers in order to attack me, catch fire and roast to ashes, in the name of Jesus.
17. Witchcraft power assign to waste my resources, die, in the name of Jesus.
18. Wicked agenda of strangers for my life break in the name of Jesus.

19. Strange king installed to humiliate and keep me captive, be dethroned and die in the name of Jesus.
20. Powers keeping me in bondage release me and die in the name of Jesus.
21. Every strongman and woman operating against me, die in the name of Jesus.
22. Powers monitoring me for evil, go blind and die, in the name of Jesus.
23. Holy Ghost Fire, burn every work of stranger in my life, in the name of Jesus.
24. Strange food in my stomach, I vomit you, in the name of Jesus.
25. Heavenly angels scatter and disgrace stubborn pursuers after my life, in the name of Jesus.
26. Every satanic opposition against my destiny scatter, in the name of Jesus.
27. Rulers of darkness in charge of my case, die in the name of Jesus.
28. Thou troubler of my Israel, your time is up, die, in the name of Jesus.
29. Spirit marriage holding me captive to spirit spouse, break, in the name of Jesus.
30. Marine powers in the water molesting me in my sleep, die in the name of Jesus.

31. Messenger of darkness on assignment to announce my obituary in the spirit, die, in the name of Jesus.
32. Rock of Ages; grind my enemy to dust, in the name of Jesus.
33. Every hidden place of the enemy, be destroyed by thunder, in the name of Jesus.
34. Dark soldiers advancing to my house in the spirit in order to kill me, die on your way, in the name of Jesus.
35. Powers holding vigil to destroy me, be destroyed in your evil act in the name of Jesus.
36. Evil command of the enemy giving me instruction on what to do, in order to destroy me, scatter in the name of Jesus.
37. Strange immigration officer monitoring me about, my life is not your candidate; die in the name of Jesus.
38. Every stronghold of darkness keeping in wait for judgment, scatter in the name of Jesus.
39. O Lord, disgrace who trust in their wealth to humiliate me, in the name of Jesus.
40. Destructive forces that vow to kill me, your time is up, die, in the name of Jesus.
41. Destructive forces that vow to burn my properties in the spirit, die, in the name of Jesus.

42. Those I enjoy fellowship with but decide to pull me down, be exposed and be disgraced, in the name of Jesus.
43. Enemies and foes that rise up to insult me and silence me, die in the name of Jesus.
44. Powers assigned to cause violence and strife in my place of work, die in the name of Jesus.
45. Powers assigned to cause sudden death in my name, die in the name of Jesus.
46. O Lord, confuse the wicked, confound their speech, in the name of Jesus.
47. O Lord, let the evil men do recoil on them, in the name of Jesus.
48. O Lord, disgrace every one that pay me evil for good, in the name of Jesus.
49. Powers assign to sow seed of grief in my soul and body die in the name of Jesus.
50. Every arrow of failure fired into my life, come out of me, backfire and consume your sender.
51. Every evil arrow fired from the pit of hell to scatter my finance, backfire in the name of Jesus.
52. Every arrow of darkness fired to scatter my marriage backfire in the name of Jesus.
53. Every arrow of darkness fired to scatter my destiny backfire, in the name of Jesus.

54. Satanic tact used to dupe people, I am not for you, scatter in the name of Jesus.
55. Any power or personality coming to me as innocent but doing evil for me in the spirit, be exposed and be disgraced in the name of Jesus.
56. Confusion of the highest order scatter the camp of my enemy in the name of Jesus.
57. Powers that want me to be lonely and afflicted die, in the name of Jesus.
58. O Lord, let death take my enemies by surprise, in the name of Jesus.
59. Powers that want me to go down to the grave, replace me and die, in the name of Jesus.
60. Every battle waged against me, scatter, in the name of Jesus.
61. Bloodthirsty agents after my life, fight yourselves until you perish, in the name of Jesus.
62. Those that hotly pursued me, shall fall down and die, in the name of Jesus.
63. Powers watching my steps in order to harm me, die in the name of Jesus.
64. I refuse and reject to fellowship with works of darkness, in the name of Jesus.
65. O Lord, bring down powers boasting they are at the top today, in the name of Jesus.

66. O Lord, deliver my feet from stumbling, let my joy be full, in the name of Jesus.
67. Sustain me O Lord, as I cast my cares on you in the name of Jesus.
68. O Lord, hear my cry in distress, convert it to laughter and joy, in the name of Jesus.
69. O Lord, exalt me where others plan to bring me down, in the name of Jesus.
70. O Lord my God, redeem my life from the hand of the wicked, in the name of Jesus.
71. I shall not be a waste like water poured out on dry sand in the name of Jesus.
72. I shall not spread my hands to idol, in the name of Jesus.
73. Evil days ahead of me, I am not your candidate, die, in the name of Jesus.
74. My destiny, wake up, arise and shine, in the name of Jesus.
75. By word of prophecy, my Lord shall hear and defend me in the day of trouble, in the name of Jesus.
76. By word of prophecy, strangers shall come out of their close places and obey me, in the name of Jesus.
77. By word of prophecy, dark strangers shall fade away in my life, in the name of Jesus.

78. By word of prophecy, my God shall avenge me and subdue my adversaries under me, in the name of Jesus.
79. Begin to thank God for what he has done in this prayer and what he will do thereafter. Do the thanksgiving for about 5 minutes.

TELLA OLAYERI

CHAPTER 2

I REBUKE DISGRACE AND SHAME

Genesis 32:26-28

26. Then the man said, "Let me go, for it is daybreak." But Jacob replied, "I will not let you go unless you bless me."

27. The man asked him, "What is your name?" "Jacob," he answered.

28. Then the man said, "Your name will no longer be Jacob, but Israel, because you have struggled with God and with humans and have overcome."

2 Kings 19:32-33

32. "Therefore this is what the LORD says concerning the king of Assyria: "'He will not enter this city or shoot an arrow here. He will not come before it with shield or build a siege ramp against it.

33. By the way that he came he will return; he will not enter this city, declares the LORD.

Job 8:21-22

21. He will yet fill your mouth with laughter and your lips with shouts of joy.

22. Your enemies will be clothed in shame, and the tents of the wicked will be no more."

PRAYER POINTS

1. I thank my God who rebuke my enemy and put them to shame, in the name of Jesus.
2. O Lord, I thank you for your protection on me, in the name of Jesus.
3. I thank my God for lifting me up when I fall, in the name of Jesus.
4. O Lord, I come before you, forgive me and put shame from me, in the name of Jesus.
5. I wear garment of forgiveness and tear garment of shame, in the name of Jesus.
6. O Lord, let your forgiveness be total upon me in the name of Jesus.
7. I cover myself with blood of Jesus against arrow of shame, in the name of Jesus.
8. I drink blood of Jesus and purge every deposit of shame and disgrace in my body, in the name of Jesus.
9. Blood of Jesus, wash me clean of shame and disgrace, in the name of Jesus.

10. Holy Spirit create conducive environment that favour progress for me, in the name of Jesus.
11. Holy Spirit, guide my footstep to truth, in the name of Jesus.
12. Holy Ghost Power, incubate my spirit man for signs and wonders, in the name of Jesus.
13. Satanic anointing that bring shame to life, dry up, in the name of Jesus.
14. My Jacob, wrestle with shame and overcome it, and let me be great in the name of Jesus.
15. Any power that wants me in the valley, I am not your candidate die in the name of Jesus.
16. O Lord, bless my struggle let my shame and disgrace be converted to blessing and promotion, in the name of Jesus.
17. O Lord, rebuke disgrace and put to shame enemies of my soul, in the name of Jesus.
18. Powers planning to shoot arrow of disgrace to me, fail woefully, in the name of Jesus.
19. Evil altar, giving power to my enemy, catch fire and roast to ashes, in the name of Jesus.
20. My enemy shall be like grass sprouting on the roof, scorched before it grows up, in the name of Jesus.
21. I shall not beg before I feed in the name of Jesus.

22. Every garment of shame and disgrace in my life, I rebuke you, catch fire and roast to ashes, in the name of Jesus.
23. O Lord, clothe my enemies with shame, in the name of Jesus.
24. Thou tent of the enemy, become desolate in the name of Jesus.
25. O Lord, slap my enemy and let them reveal evil plan against me, in the name of Jesus.
26. O Lord, let my enemy regret the day they were born, in the name of Jesus.
27. As a cloud vanishes and is gone, let my shame vanish in the name of Jesus.
28. O Lord, let my enemy wither more quickly than grass, let them become nothing, in the name of Jesus.
29. O Lord, let my enemy do nothing and be useless, in the name of Jesus.
30. O Lord, perform miracles that cannot be counted in my life in the name of Jesus.
31. My father and my God, fill my lips with shouts of joy, in the name of Jesus.
32. My father and my God, fill my mouth with laughter, in the name of Jesus.
33. Powers that vow to kill me and divide my garments die, in the name of Jesus.

34. Powers pursuing me from my place of birth in order to destroy me, die in the name of Jesus.
35. Angels of God, be my armies, subdue and destroy my stubborn pursuers, in the name of Jesus.
36. O Lord, cover the face of my stubborn pursuer with deep darkness, in the name of Jesus.
37. O God, disgrace enemies that gathered to testify against me, in the name of Jesus.
38. O Lord, now is the day of trouble, deliver me in the name of Jesus.
39. Stubborn pursuers wielding axe at me, die with your axe, in the name of Jesus.
40. O Lord, burn down the sanctuary of enemies after my soul, in the name of Jesus.
41. O Lord, let the covenant of "Thou shall not die" be upon me, in the name of Jesus.
42. Violence activities in dark places against me, scatter in the name of Jesus.
43. O Lord, let every power that refuse to turn back from pursuing me, summersault and die, in the name of Jesus.
44. Every dragon against my hand-work, your time is up, die in the name of Jesus.
45. Stubborn pursuer after my life become chaff before the wind and be blown out, in the name of Jesus.

46. Father Lord, draw out your spear, stop the stubborn pursuers that vow to deal with me, in the name of Jesus.
47. Father Lord, let the wicked turn back and meet double failure, in the name of Jesus.
48. Powers assign to multiply the troubles of my heart, die in the name of Jesus.
49. Enemies that pray my flesh and heart to fail, you are a liar, your prayer shall fail you, in the name of Jesus.
50. Powers that want me to perish in the journey of life, die in the name of Jesus.
51. Unfaithful around me be exposed and be disgraced, in the name of Jesus.
52. I shall not retreat in disgrace, but face enemies of my soul and defeat them, in the name of Jesus.
80. O Lord, rebuke the enemy, who are arrogant, my God says "Boast no more", for you shall fail in the name of Jesus.
81. O Lord, rebuke the enemy, who are the wicked, my God says, "Do not lift up your hands", for you shall fail in the name of Jesus.
53. O Lord, this is the appointed time to save me from the hands of the wicked, save me, in the name of Jesus.

54. Every adversary against my career, scatter, in the name of Jesus.
55. Rise up O God, and defend me to the last, in the name of Jesus.
56. O Lord, those afflicted in my environment by power of darkness, heal them, in the name of Jesus.
57. O Lord, do not hand over my life to the enemy, in the name of Jesus.
58. O God arise, let forces that join together against me flee in terror, in the name of Jesus.
59. Every false witness that comes forward to witness against me in the spirit, be disgraced in the name of Jesus.
60. Stubborn pursuers after me, I beat you, and cast you out as dirt in the street, in the name of Jesus.
82. Enemies that trust in their chariots and horses, fall down and die in the name of Jesus.
61. My stubborn pursuers turn your step to everlasting ruin, in the name of Jesus
62. Powers on assignment to send me to jail, die in the name of Jesus.
63. Powers on assignment to burn my properties and naked me, you are a failure, die in the name of Jesus.

64. I take refuge in the Lord from my foes, and they scattered in the name of Jesus
65. I subdue my stubborn pursuers and kill them, in the name of Jesus.
66. I receive power to pursue, overtake and possess my possession from the enemy, in the name of Jesus.
67. O Lord, break the needs of the monster in the waters, after my life, in the name of Jesus.
68. Power chasing me from springs and streams of God, die in the name of Jesus.
69. Lord Jesus, free me from the anguish of the wicked, in the name of Jesus.
70. Earthquake of deliverance of the Lord, locate me and deliver me, in the name of Jesus.
71. Rivers of joy and breakthrough flow into my life, in the name of Jesus.
72. O Lord, be my redeemer, redeem my life today, in the name of Jesus.
73. My hope in the Lord shall not be dashed to pieces.
74. Enemies shall not triumph over me, in the name of Jesus.
75. Powers that make me hate instruction of God, come out of me, in the name of Jesus.

76. O Lord, create wide boundary and demarcation between me and my pursuers, in the name of Jesus.
77. O Lord, silence enemies expecting to mock me, in the name of Jesus.
78. O Lord, give signs that my enemies are defeated, in the name of Jesus.
79. O Lord, don't be silent of my situation, deliver me from stubborn pursuers in the name of Jesus.
80. O Lord, tie big rod in the legs of my stubborn pursuers for them to fall and rise no more in the name of Jesus
81. O Lord tie big stone in the waist of my enemy so that they don't overtake me.
82. O Lord give me permanent deliverance from the hands of my stubborn pursuer in the name of Jesus
83. Enemy shall not trample me to the ground, in the name of Jesus.

CHAPTER 3

O LORD SILENCE POWERS OPPOSING PROSPERITY IN MY LIFE

Numbers 10:35

35. Whenever the ark set out, Moses said, "Rise up, LORD! May your enemies be scattered; may your foes flee before you."

Psalm 3:7-8

7. Arise, LORD! Deliver me, my God! Strike all my enemies on the jaw; break the teeth of the wicked.

8. From the LORD comes deliverance. May your blessing be on your people.

Psalm 40:13-15

13. Be pleased to save me, LORD; come quickly, LORD, to help me.

14. May all who want to take my life be put to shame and confusion; may all who desire my ruin be turned back in disgrace.

15. May those who say to me, "Aha! Aha!" be appalled at their own shame.

PRAYER POINTS

1. I thank my God, for silencing opposition against me, in the name of Jesus.
2. I thank my God, who gives his angels charge over my life, in the name of Jesus.
3. I thank my God, who blesses me in the midst of my enemies, in the name of Jesus.
4. O Lord, I come before you, let all sins in my life vanish and be forgiven, in the name of Jesus.
5. O Lord, let all ungodliness in my life, disappear, in the name of Jesus.
6. I confess my sins and repent of it (do it), in the name of Jesus.
7. I plead blood of Jesus upon my prosperity in the name of Jesus.
8. I drink blood of Jesus to strengthen me and put me in good shape, in the name of Jesus.
9. Holy Spirit come as dew and refresh me, let prosperity blossom in my life, in the name of Jesus.
10. Holy Spirit, fill me afresh in the name of Jesus.
11. Holy spirit, I stretch my hand of fellowship to you, receive me, in the name of Jesus.

12. O Lord arise, let my enemy scatter in the name of Jesus.
13. O Lord let my foes flee before me in the name of Jesus.
14. I receive fresh fire to challenge and defeat powers opposing my prosperity, in the name of Jesus.
15. O Lord arise, be angry with powers opposing my prosperity, in the name of Jesus.
16. O Lord, come quickly to my situation and silence powers opposing prosperity in my life, in the name of Jesus.
17. O Lord, let those who oppose and want to put me to shame, be disgraced in the name of Jesus.
18. O Lord, let those who seek to take my life, die unnatural death in my place, in the name of Jesus.
19. O Lord, let those who desire my ruin be turned back in disgrace, in the name of Jesus.
20. Those who imagine the worst for me, shall fail woefully in the name of Jesus.
21. Powers firing arrow at me to be downcast and weak, shall reap double failure, in the name of Jesus.
22. Powers assigned to introduce holes in the pocket in my life, die in the name of Jesus.

23. O Lord, put my adversaries to shame in the name of Jesus.
24. Prosperity eating and drinking demons, assigned from pit of hell against me, die in the name of Jesus.
25. Powers campaigning frustration to render me useless die in the name of Jesus.
26. Every evil altar consulted to oppose my glory, catch fire and roast to ashes, in the name of Jesus.
27. Rulers of darkness giving me evil command die in the name of Jesus.
28. Rulers of darkness upon my life, scatter in the name of Jesus.
29. Every dream of failure, be converted to success, in the name of Jesus.
30. Every spirit that collect and spend my money on my behalf in the spirit, die, in the name of Jesus.
31. My money tied down in the spirit, be released unto me, in the name of Jesus.
32. Any charm assign to suffocate my wealth, die in the name of Jesus.
33. O Lord, surprise me, let fountains open in the valley to favour me, in the name of Jesus.
34. I enter and recover my property in satanic warehouse in the name of Jesus.

35. Satanic warehouse where my assets are kept in the spirit, catch fire and roast to ashes, in the name of Jesus.
36. Satanic bankers in charge of my finance, die in the name of Jesus.
37. Powers opposing prosperity in my life, die, in the name of Jesus.
38. Satanic network that lure me to wilderness, catch fire and roast to ashes, in the name of Jesus.
39. Every hand of demotion stretched to receive me in order to destroy me, wither in the name of Jesus.
40. Network of Satan that rubbish life lose your hold upon my life, in the name of Jesus.
41. Property of evil stranger in my life, catch fire and roast to ashes, in the name of Jesus.
42. Seed of darkness, planted in my life, wither and die, in the name of Jesus.
43. Spirit of destruction that vow to scatter the journey of my life, your time is up, go blind, in the name of Jesus.
44. Anything planted in my life to naked me, wither and die, in the name of Jesus.
45. Powers that hold the key of my destiny, release it today, and die, in the name of Jesus.

46. Every bitter water flowing to my life, dry up, in the name of Jesus.
47. Bitter water assigned for me in the spirit, dry up, in the name of Jesus.
48. Water of sorrow, assign for me to bath with, dry up in the name of Jesus.
49. Every bitter water assign for my household, dry up, in the name of Jesus.
50. Power of sin harvesting my fortune and sucking me dry, die, in the name of Jesus.
51. Let every satanic transaction against my destiny scatter, in the name of Jesus.
52. Satanic network controlling my affairs in the spirit, scatter and catch fire, in the name of Jesus.
53. Every advance payment I do in the spirit, be nullified in the name of Jesus.
54. O Lord, turn my wilderness to pool of water, in the name of Jesus.
55. O Lord, let my dry places spring out water, in the name of Jesus.
56. My father and my God, make my wilderness a pool of water, and my dry land springs in the name of Jesus.
57. Powers forcing me to do profitless hard-work die, in the name of Jesus.

58. Every custom and tradition that keep me away from God, I reject you in the name of Jesus.
59. My wealth depart from evil altar, in the name of Jesus.
60. Period of frustration and confusion in my life, expire in the name of Jesus.
61. Anointing of demotion on my head, dry up, in the name of Jesus.
62. O Lord, reverse period of wilderness in my life to prosperity in the name of Jesus.
63. O Lord, reverse period of wilderness in my life from insults to result, in the name of Jesus.
64. O Lord, reverse period of wilderness in my life from ridicule to miracle, in the name of Jesus.
65. O Lord, reverse period of wilderness in my life from scars to stars of glory, in the name of Jesus.
66. O Lord, reverse period of wilderness in my life from weakness to strength, in the name of Jesus.
67. O Lord, reverse period of wilderness in my life from disgrace to favour and grace in the name of Jesus.
68. O Lord, reverse period of wilderness in my life from frustration to fulfillment and fruitfulness, in the name of Jesus.

69. O Lord, reverse period of wilderness in my life from failure to success and joy, in the name of Jesus.
70. O Lord, reverse period of wilderness in my life from defeat to victory, in the name of Jesus.
71. O God arise, convert defeat awaiting me to victory, in the name of Jesus.
72. I shall not engage in profitless hardwork, in the name of Jesus.
73. Enemies shall not rejoice over me in the name of Jesus.
74. I shall not labour under the spirit of failure, in the name of Jesus.
75. Today, I walk away from powers assign to lead me to wilderness, in the name of Jesus.
76. I recover back every good thing sin destroy in my life, in the name of Jesus.
77. I shall breakthrough, not break down in the journey of life, in the name of Jesus.
78. O Lord, plant my destiny by the rivers of success and prosperity, in the name of Jesus.
79. O Lord, I stretch my hands unto you, lead me to people that will bless me, in the name of Jesus.

CHAPTER 4

I OVERCOME POWERS OLDER THAN ME

Leviticus 26:6-8

6. I will grant peace in the land, and you will lie down and no one will make you afraid. I will remove wild beasts from the land, and the sword will not pass through your country.

7. You will pursue your enemies, and they will fall by the sword before you.

8. Five of you will chase a hundred, and a hundred of you will chase ten thousand, and your enemies will fall by the sword before you.

Psalm 144:1-2

1. Praise be to the LORD my Rock, who trains my hands for war, my fingers for battle.

2. He is my loving God and my fortress, my stronghold and my deliverer, my shield, in whom I take refuge, who subdues peoples under me.

Psalm 125:1-3

1. Those who trust in the LORD are like Mount Zion, which cannot be shaken but endures forever.

2. As the mountains surround Jerusalem, so the LORD surrounds his people both now and forevermore.

3. The scepter of the wicked will not remain over the land allotted to the righteous, for then the righteous might use their hands to do evil.

PRAYER POINTS

1. I thank you Lord for spirit of revelation you give me to know the battles ahead of me, in the name of Jesus.
2. O Lord, I thank you for firing up my prayer altar, to destroy powers that are older than me, causing trouble, in the name of Jesus.
3. I thank my God, who trains my hands for war, my fingers for battle, in the name of Jesus.
4. O Lord, lay hands of mercy and deliverance upon me in the name of Jesus.
5. O Lord my God, have mercy upon me in the name of Jesus.
6. O Lord, forgive me every sin that make ancestral powers in my lineage to supervise me in the name of Jesus.

7. Blood of Jesus, flow from my head to my toes and silence ancestral powers monitoring my family in the name of Jesus.
8. O Lord, break down and mold me over with blood of Jesus.
9. I drink blood of Jesus, to flush me of impurity in the name of Jesus.
10. Anti-revival spirit in my life, come out of me and die, in the name of Jesus.
11. Spirit of holiness, that will make me subdue powers older than me, come upon me in the name of Jesus.
12. O Lord, let spiritual gifts that are dead in my life, receive life, in the name of Jesus.
13. Arrows of impatience fired against me, backfire, in the name of Jesus.
14. Power around me that hates progress die in the name of Jesus.
15. When I lie down enemy will not overpower me in the name of Jesus.
16. Sword of darkness, raised at me, break in the name of Jesus.
17. Every enemy that turn against me I cut you to pieces with sword of God, in the name of Jesus.
18. I chase my enemies in the spirit, I overtake them, and slaughter them, in the name of Jesus.

19. Powers older than me, assign to empty my treasure your time is up, die in the name of Jesus.
20. Powers older than me, assign to kill me, die, in the name of Jesus.
21. Evil altar of my father's house monitoring me since the day I was born, catch fire and roast to ashes, in the name of Jesus.
22. Masquerade powers of my father's house, die, in the name of Jesus.
23. Ancestral shrine of my father's house, leave me alone and die, in the name of Jesus.
24. Wicked powers of my father's house, older than me, I trust in the Lord, therefore die, in the name of Jesus.
25. As the mountains surround Jerusalem, so shall the Lord surround me forever, in the name of Jesus.
26. O Lord, make my home holy devoid of wicked deposit, in the name of Jesus.
27. Every yoke troubling my generation before I was born, break in the name of Jesus.
28. Powers that put my family line in captivity die, in the name of Jesus.
29. I reject wilderness of life, in the name of Jesus.
30. Spiritual blindness making me thread wrong way of life, expire in the name of Jesus.

31. Every satanic baggage in my possession, I discard you and burn you to ashes, in the name of Jesus.
32. Oppressor of my soul, pierce your heart with the sword you hold, in the name of Jesus.
33. O Lord, let the plot of the wicked against me scatter in the name of Jesus.
34. Thou enemy of my soul be clothed with shame and confusion, in the name of Jesus.
35. O Lord, let the way of the oppressor be dark and slippery, never to catch up with me, in the name of Jesus.
36. Every wickedness of the wicked against my life, be terminated, in the name of Jesus.
37. Fire of deliverance, catch up with oppressor tormenting my life in the name of Jesus.
38. Goliath of darkness of my father's house assign to waste me, be wasted, in the name of Jesus.
39. Goliath of darkness of my mother's house assign to waste me, be wasted, in the name of Jesus.
40. Goliath of darkness of my In-law's house assign to waste me, be wasted, in the name of Jesus.
41. O Lord, let the sword enemy fashion against me turn against them, in the name of Jesus.

42. Every evil bird flying to cause harm in my life, fall down and die, in the name of Jesus.
43. Heavenly whirlwind, sweep away the wicked, in the name of Jesus.
44. My fear, fall upon my adversaries, and silence them, in the name of Jesus.
45. Desert spirit, in my father's house, tormenting me with arrow of poverty, enough is enough, I fire back the evil arrow to consume you.
46. Oppressors of my soul, assign to bury my talent, your time is up, die, in the name of Jesus.
47. Thou oppressor that trouble my Israel, my God shall trouble you today, in the name of Jesus.
48. Powers counting days and time to terminate me be terminated, in the name of Jesus.
49. Every destruction enemy prepare for me, be consumed by it, in the name of Jesus.
50. O Lord let consuming smoke go out of your nostril and consume every plantation growing in the garden of my life.
51. Holy Ghost, fire arrow and scatter enemies assign to oppress me in the spirit.
52. Powers blocking my breakthrough from shining, enough is enough, die in the name of Jesus.

53. Powers older than me in my father's house, tormenting and troubling us, die in the name of Jesus.
54. Oppressors in my dream, paralyze and die, in the name of Jesus.
55. Powers that tag themselves, "Kill and go" in my father's house, I am not your candidate, die in the name of Jesus.
56. Strongman of my father's house keeping me busy with unprofitable business in order to make me a failure, die in the name of Jesus.
57. Stubborn pursuers that refuse to let me go, I am not your candidate, die in the name of Jesus.
58. Stubborn pursuers that vow to pursue me till I enter grave, leave me alone and die in the name of Jesus.
59. Quencher of anointing that vow I will not make it in life, you are not my God, die in the name of Jesus.
60. I fire arrow of destruction against my enemy and destroy them in the name of Jesus.
61. Witchcraft powers planting evil seeds in the garden of my life, die in the name of Jesus.
62. Let the seed of witchcraft powers wither and die, in the name of Jesus.

63. Power in my sleep that vow to poison me in my sleep, my God rebuke you, die in the name of Jesus.
64. I receive power to beat my oppressors to smallness as the dust before the wind, in the name of Jesus.
65. Oppressors that boast, "Where is your God" my God is "I AM that I AM", therefore be put to shame, in the name of Jesus.
66. Whirlwind of God, blow away and paralyze oppressors of my life, in the name of Jesus.
67. Oppressors of my soul shall fall before me, in the name of Jesus.
68. Every satanic agent among my friends, be exposed and be disgraced in the name of Jesus.
69. O Lord, let every oppressor be put to shame, in the name of Jesus.
70. O Lord, revive my finance and let my destiny experience turn around breakthrough, in the name of Jesus.
71. O Lord, let me see my desire upon my enemies, in the name of Jesus.
72. My hanging breakthrough, I set you free, locate me by fire in the name of Jesus.
73. My enemy shall not rejoice over me in the name of Jesus.

74. By word of prophecy, I speak life into the dry bones and evil valley to disappear, in the name of Jesus.
75. By word of prophecy, I speak light into my dark areas, in the name of Jesus.
76. By word of prophecy, I speak destruction to stagnancy and failure in the name of Jesus.
77. By word of prophecy, I command every destructive forces assign against my life to die, in the name of Jesus.
78. By word of prophecy, my life is preserved and secured from oppression, in the name of Jesus.
79. O Lord, wear everyone in my family with garment of righteousness, in the name of Jesus.
80. By word of prophecy, my enemies shall bow and leave in shame, in the name of Jesus.

CHAPTER 5

WITCHCRAFT POWER ASSIGN TO EMPTY ME SHALL FAIL

Isaiah 43:1-2

1. But now, this is what the LORD says he who created you, Jacob, he who formed you, Israel: "Do not fear, for I have redeemed you; I have summoned you by name; you are mine.

2. When you pass through the waters, I will be with you; and when you pass through the rivers, they will not sweep over you. When you walk through the fire, you will not be burned; the flames will not set you ablaze.

Psalm 144:13-14

13. Our barns will be filled with every kind of provision. Our sheep will increase by thousands, by tens of thousands in our fields;

14. Our oxen will draw heavy loads. There will be no breaching of walls, no going into captivity, no cry of distress in our streets.

Psalm 128:5-6

5. May the LORD bless you from Zion; may you see the prosperity of Jerusalem all the days of your life.

6. May you live to see your children's children, peace be on Israel.

PRAYER POINTS

1. I thank my God, who disgraced emptier in my life, in the name of Jesus.
2. I thank you O Lord, for your mercy and protection upon my life, in the name of Jesus.
3. I thank God who makes me live above emptier assigned to destroy my hope and joy, in the name of Jesus.
4. Lord Jesus, lay your hand of forgiveness upon me and forgive me, in the name of Jesus.
5. O Lord, let me see your face, forgive me, in the name of Jesus.
6. I reject powers dedicating sin to me, in the name of Jesus.
7. Blood of Jesus, flow around me, in the name of Jesus.
8. I drink blood of Jesus to make me whole, energize me against principalities and power, in the name of Jesus.

9. Blood of Jesus, flow in my vein, in the name of Jesus.
10. O Lord, bless me from Zion and let emptier around me be empty, in the name of Jesus.
11. Witchcraft emptier in the corridor of my life, surrender and die, in the name of Jesus.
12. Witchcraft emptier that vow, he will empty me, you are a liar, die, in the name of Jesus.
13. Witchcraft emptier that refuse to leave my prosperity, your time is up, die in the name of Jesus.
14. Witchcraft emptier fighting against the restoration of my fortune, go blind, in the name of Jesus.
15. Witchcraft emptier, assign to empty to empty my barn, die, in the name of Jesus.
16. Witchcraft emptier working against increase of my prosperity, your time is up, die, in the name of Jesus.
17. Witchcraft emptier, wishing me cry in my undertaking, I am not your candidate, die in the name of Jesus.
18. Flood of darkness assign against me dry up, in the name of Jesus.
19. Dark waters assign against my destiny in the spirit dry up in the name of Jesus.

20. Fire of God, consume stubborn pursuers after my life, in the name of Jesus.
21. Flames of God, set ablaze works of darkness targeted at me in the name of Jesus.
22. Powers assigned to hold me back, I am not your candidate, die in the name of Jesus.
23. Powers that want me to live in regret, your time is up, die in the name of Jesus.
24. My virtues in the warehouse of darkness, I possess you in the name of Jesus.
25. I shall not be plundered any more, in the name of Jesus.
26. O Lord, enrich me with your gift, in the name of Jesus.
27. O Lord, deliver me from deadly arrows of the wicked, in the name of Jesus.
28. Every prison yard prepared for me, catch fire and roast to ashes, in the name of Jesus.
29. Commanders of darkness assign to kill me, die in my place in the name of Jesus.
30. Powers assigned to naked me, I am not your candidate, die, in the name of Jesus.
31. Envoys of darkness with evil mission to demote me, die in the name of Jesus.
32. Every curse of rise and fall pronounced against me, backfire in the name of Jesus.

33. O Lord, let the enemies of my breakthrough run mad and die, in the name of Jesus
34. Desert spirit, that scatter and destroy efforts that is after my star, die, in the name of Jesus.
35. Security guards, that pull me back at the edge of breakthrough, die, in the name of Jesus.
36. Every dark record of my business, catch fire and roast to ashes, in the name of Jesus.
37. Every mountain of darkness firing arrow against my success, catch fire and roast to ashes, in the name of Jesus.
38. Every stone of darkness stationed between me and my breakthrough, break, in the name of Jesus.
39. Power of sin, stealing from me, lose your hold upon me, in the name of Jesus.
40. Stagnancy, I am not your victim, release me and die, in the name of Jesus.
41. Seed of darkness planted in my life to make me remain stagnant, wither and die, in the name of Jesus.
42. Satanic prophecy from my father's house against my finance, backfire and scatter, in the name of Jesus.
43. Evil burial against my finance, your time is up, catch fire and roast to ashes, in the name of Jesus.

44. I shall not fish in foul water of life, in the name of Jesus.
45. Powers waiting to harm me at the edge of breakthrough die in the name of Jesus.
46. Powers waiting to seize my bag of breakthrough at the edge of breakthrough die in the name of Jesus.
47. Evil food prepared for me, before my breakthrough will appear, catch fire and roast to ashes in the name of Jesus.
48. Power assign to run me down at the point of breakthrough, your time is up, die in the name of Jesus.
49. Witchcraft embargo that stand between me and breakthrough, break, in the name of Jesus.
50. Marine witchcraft that held me back from reaching my breakthrough, die in the name of Jesus.
51. Arrow of God, locate the head of powers hindering my success to come to fulfillment, in the name of Jesus.
52. Inherited darkness, holding me back from my breakthrough, clear away, in the name of Jesus.
53. Inherited failure from my father's house, that refuse to let me experience breakthrough, expire, in the name of Jesus.

54. Inherited battle that bring losses, troubling my life, scatter in the name of Jesus.
55. Sudden death, come upon powers hindering my breakthrough in the name of Jesus.
56. Strange powers that divert my miracle elsewhere, enough is enough, die in the name of Jesus.
57. Power singing song of backwardness to my ear, you are a failure, die, in the name of Jesus.
58. Any hand, pulling me from reaching my goal, wither, in the name of Jesus.
59. Every road junction waiting to swallow my wealth, catch fire and roast to ashes, in the name of Jesus.
60. Witchcraft agenda to scatter my finance, shall not see the light of the day, in the name of Jesus.
61. Spirit of emptier in my life assign to scatter what I gather, die, in the name of Jesus.
62. O Lord, deliver me where I need deliverance, in the name of Jesus.
63. Satanic decree upon my prosperity, be revoked, in the name of Jesus.
64. The hand of the wicked shall not prosper over me, in the name of Jesus.
65. Every yoke of disappointment at the edge of breakthrough, break in the name of Jesus.

66. Every yoke of sudden death of helpers at the edge of breakthrough, break, in the name of Jesus.
67. Every yoke of poverty that scatter breakthrough at the edge of solution, break in the name of Jesus.
68. Every yoke that kill effort at the edge of breakthrough, break in the name of Jesus.
69. O Lord, let people gather to celebrate me, in the name of Jesus.
70. My season of profit and abundance, appear, in the name of Jesus.
71. Anointing to pray and profit, come upon me, in the name of Jesus.
72. My doors of supernatural promotion, open by fire, in the name of Jesus.
73. Miracles of explosive prosperity that swallow poverty, my life is available enter and do wonders, in the name of Jesus.
74. O Lord, I am determined to succeed this year, help me to forge ahead, in the name of Jesus.
75. I decree against evil barricades against my breakthrough to catch fire and roast to ashes, in the name of Jesus.
76. By word of prophecy, my God shall open rivers in high places to water the garden of my life in the name of Jesus

77. By word of prophecy, I shall operate at the top only and not below, in the name of Jesus.
78. I shall not be a failure, key of success shall not depart from my hands, in the name of Jesus.
79. Oh my destiny, sign contract with heaven and be blessed, in the name of Jesus.
80. Supernatural promotion that will turn me to eagle of wealth, take place now, in the name of Jesus.
81. My heaven, open and bless my breakthrough, in the name of Jesus.
82. My wealth accumulated in strange tree, vomit it by fire in the name of Jesus.
83. Holy Ghost break every battle that swallow my destiny, in the name of Jesus.
84. My buried destiny, in the spirit, I exhume you, come forth, in the name of Jesus.
85. My destiny, swallowed by marine spirit, be vomited in the name of Jesus.
86. My destiny, buried in the river bank, be released unto me in the name of Jesus.
87. My breakthrough in the cage of enemy, my God set you free today, escape and locate me, in the name of Jesus.

YOU HAVE BATTLES TO WIN
TRY THESE BOOKS

1. COMMAND THE DAY: DAILY PRAYER BOOK

Each day of the week is loaded with meanings and divine assurance. God did not create each day of the week for the fun of it. Blessings, success, gifts, resources, hopes, portfolios, duties, rights, prophecies, warnings and challenges, are loaded in each day.

Do you know the language, command or decree you can use to claim what belongs to you in each day of the week? Do you know in Christendom, Monday can be equated to one of the days of creation in Genesis chapter one? Do you know creation lasted for six days and God rested on the seventh day? What day of the week can Christian equate as the first day of the week, if we follow Christian calendar? What day can we call day seven?

This book shall give insight to these questions. It shall explain how you can command each day of the week according to creation in the book of Genesis chapter one.

Above all, you shall exercise your right and claim what is hidden in each day of the week.
Check for this in **COMMAND THE DAY: DAILY PRAYER BOOK**

2. **PRAYER TO REMEMBER DREAMS**

A lot of people are passing through this spiritual epidemic on a daily basis. Their dream life is epileptic, having no ability to remember all dreams they dream, or sometimes forget everything entirely. This is nothing but spiritual havoc you need to erase from your spiritual record.
The answer to every form of spiritual blackout caused by spiritual erasers is found in, **PRAYER TO REMEMBER DREAMS**

3. **100% CONFESSIONS AND PROPHECIES TO LOCATE HELPERS AND HELPERS TO LOCATE YOU**

This is a wonderful book on confessions and prophecies to locate helpers and helpers to locate you. It is a prayer book loaded with over two thousand (2,000) prayer points.

The book unravels how to locate unknown helpers, prayers to arrest mind of helpers and prayers for manifestation after encounter with helpers.

4. ANOINTING FOR ELEVENTH HOUR HELP: HOPE AND HELP FOR YOUR TURBULENT TIMES

This book tells much of what to do at injury hour called eleventh hour. When you read and use this book as prescribed fear shall vanish in your life when pursuing a project, career or contract.

5. PRAYER TO LOCATE HELPERS AND HELPERS TO LOCATE YOU

Our divine helper is God. He created us to be together and be of help to one another. In the midst of no help we lost out, ending our journey in the wilderness.

There are keys assign to open right doors of life. You need right key to locate your helpers. Enough is enough; of suffering in silence.

With this book, you shall locate your helpers while your helpers shall locate you.

6. FIRE FOR FIRE PART ONE: (PRAYER BOOK BOOK 1)

This prayer book is fast at answering spiritual problems. It is a bulldozer prayer book, full of prayers all through. It is highly recommended for night vigil. Testimonies are pouring in daily from users of this book across the world!

7. PRAYER FOR FRUIT OF THE WOMB: EXPECTING MOTHERS

This prayer book is children magnet. By faith and believe in God Almighty, as soon as you use this book open doors to child bearing shall be yours. Amen

8. PRAYER FOR PREGNANT WOMEN: WITH ALL CHRISTIAN NAMES AND MEANINGS

This is a spiritual prayer book loaded with prayers of solution for pregnant women. As soon as you take in, the prayers you shall pray from day one of conception to the day of delivery are written in this book.

9. WARFARE IN THE OFFICE: PRAYER TO SILENCE TOUGH TIMES IN OFFICE

It is high time you pray prayers of power must change hands in office. Use this book and liberate yourself from every form of office yoke.

10. MY MARRIAGE SHALL NOT BREAK: THE SECRET TO LOVE AND MARRIAGE THAT LASTS

Marriage is corner piece of life, happiness and joy. You need to hold it tight and guide it from wicked intruders and destroyer of homes.

11. VICTORY OVER SATANIC HOUSE PART ONE: RIDDING YOUR HOME OF SPIRITUAL DARKNESS

Are you a tenant, Land lord bombarded left and right, front and back by wicked people around you?
With this book you shall be liberated from the hooks of the enemy.

12. DICTIONARY OF DREAMS: THE DREAM INTERPRETATION

TELLA OLAYERI

DICTIONARY WITH SYMBOLS, SIGNS, AND MEANINGS

This is a must book for every home. It gives accurate details to about **10,000 (Ten thousand) dreams and interpretations,** written in alphabetical order for quick reference and easy digestion. The book portrays spiritual revelations with sound prophetic guidelines. It is loaded with Biblical references and violent prayers.
Ask for yours today.

For Further Enquiries Contact
**THE AUTHOR
EVANGELIST TELLA OLAYERI**
**P.O. Box 1872 Shomolu Lagos.
Tel: 08023583168**

FROM AUTHOR'S DESK

BEFORE YOU GO

Hello,

Thank you for purchasing this book. Would you consider posting a review about this book? In addition to providing feedback and arousing others into Christ's bosom, reviews can help other customers to know about the book.

Please take a minute to leave a review on this book.

I would appreciate that!

Thank you in advance, for your review and your patronage!!

Feel free to drop us your prayer request. We will join faith with you and God's power will be released in your life and issue in question.

http://tellaolayeri.com/prayerrequest.php

NOTE: You can get all my books from my website http://tellaolayeri.com

GOOD NEWS!!!

My audiobook is now available, to get one visit acx.com and search **"Tella Olayeri."**

Brethren, to be loaded and reloaded visit: amazon.com/author/tellaolayeri for a full spiritual sojourn for my books.

Thanks.

Printed in Great Britain
by Amazon